101 Fast, Good, Cheap Hacks to Writing a KILLER Sales Letter

By Jack Turk

www.101FastGoodCheapHacks.com

The author and publisher of this book and the associated materials have used their best efforts in preparing this material. The author and publisher make no representations or warranties with respect to the accuracy, applicability, fitness, or completeness of the contents of this material. They disclaim any warranties expressed or implied, merchantability, or fitness for any particular purpose. The author and publisher shall in no event be held liable for any loss or other damages, including but not limited to special, incidental, consequential, or other damages. If you have any doubts about anything, the advice of a competent professional should be sought.

This material contains elements protected under International and Federal Copyright laws and treaties. Any unauthorized reprint or use of this material is prohibited.

The great Gary Halbert said, "Every business problem can be solved with a great sales letter."

However, short cuts to writing great sales letters are hard to find.

We all know there is no avoiding the hard work.

But as a first step, rather than trying to get through 400 pages of the Robert Collier Letter Book, I highly recommend Jack Turk's 101 Fast, Good, Cheap Hacks to Writing a KILLER Sales Letter to get your juices flowing.

It's one of those books that you can turn to any page and get a useful tidbit or rule of thumb to help you with your sales letters.

Then there's more than enough time to do the hard work equipped with Jack's "101."

-Brian Kurtz, Titans Marketing LLC

TABLE OF CONTENTS

THE MYTH OF "FAST, GOOD, CHEAP - PICK TWO"

I first heard this statement years ago at a technical documentation conference - the speaker expressed it as the "golden rule of project management" and it went like this:

With every project, you have three key things to juggle: time, cost, and quality. Or, in simpler terms: fast, cheap, good. And with every project you get to pick two items.

- You can make something fast and cheap, but it won't be good.
- You can make something fast and good, but it won't be cheap.
- You can make something cheap and good, but it won't be fast.

That's the core premise. And to a great degree, it holds true with just about every task and project you take on.

But don't let this kind of thinking hold you back. There are ways to get stuff done where all three can happen simultaneously.

The key to doing this is with systems and templates and - more to the point of this book - HACKS.

THIS BOOK ANSWERS A VERY SPECIFIC PROBLEM:

Let's say your task/goal is to write a KILLER sales letter (or blog post or email or some other piece of sales copy).

Over my years as a professional copywriter for a wide range of clients (attorneys, doctors, dentists, small business owners, big businesses, coaches, and even magicians) I've discovered a lot of short cuts, templates, questions, models, key thoughts – HACKS - to help me get my copy projects finished.

Every one of these hacks has worked for me in more than one of my own businesses – as a magician, as an info-entrepreneur, and as a hired-gun copywriter who has sold millions of dollars' worth of products and services.

In this book, I'm sharing with you a boatload of hacks – some very short and concise, others with a bit more description – to make to crossing that finish line as quickly and effectively as possible.

Again, each one chosen with the aim of Fast. Cheap. Good.

Let's get started.

NOTE: Credit for many of these hacks goes to a lineage of great writers, mentors, and coaches – including John Caples, Dan Kennedy, Dave Dee, John Carlton, and a bunch of others. I've learned from the best over the years and I continue to grow by standing on the shoulders of giants.

BEFORE YOU START WRITING

WRITING

(Hacks 1-6)

1. SET A HARD DEADLINE

Many years ago, when I was working as a Technical Writer at a Boston tech firm, I scored a small side gig as a news reporter for a local paper.

My gig was simple - attend the monthly Assemblymen Meeting, take notes, and write up a story for the paper to print. Typical stories involved Farmer Matson and his request to build a fence 5 feet longer than code allowed... etc. etc. etc.

The meetings ended typically between 9PM-10PM.

The story was due at 6AM the next morning.

I would dash home, fire up my PC, and pound out the story so I could get the diskette to the paper in time for the daily run. At first it was a bit rough... and I dragged on late more than once. But once I got the hang of it, I could bang out that story in under an hour easy.

The reason - I had a HARD deadline.

There wasn't time to futz around with it.... go off in other directions... imagine other possible takes on a topic... none of that. There was time to crank out a draft, do a quick spell-check/edit, and print that puppy out.

That's the kind of mindset and mental toughness you CAN develop when you have a DEADLINE to work to. Be brutal regarding deadlines. On every project.

Deadlines are WONDERFUL things – so set a HARD Deadline and hold yourself to it.

2. COMMIT TO DONE

Here's the most critical and important element of every sales letter, email, blog post, book, or any other bit of copy...

Get it DONE!

Commit to DONE. Finish that sales letter. Launch that website. Set up your Google Adwords account.

There's magic at the finish line.

Because any project you don't finish, won't make you money - whether it's a new routine, a new salesletter, or a new website you want to have in place to promote your biz.

<u>Set a date. Get serious. Get it done.</u>

3. REJECT "THE MYTH OF PERFECT"

As a kid, I loved those wonderful stories of the ancient Norse Gods, the world of Asgard and the tales of Balder the Brave, Odin the One-Eyed King, and Loki the Trickster.

Myths can be fun, but here's a myth that could cost your business serious change:

** The Myth of Perfect **

It's a dangerous myth because I'm inherently a perfectionist. I want to make sure everything is "just-so" before I send out a sales letter or a postcard or a website.

You can always make your writing better. You can spend years and years and years and years tweaking your stuff. Instead, focus hard on saying what you want to say as fast and as clearly as you can.

You have to send it out to make the sale.

As we said back in the old days at Microsoft, "If you don't ship it, you can't sell it."

And this is a great quote from DaVinci: "Great art is never finished, only abandoned."

You will never finish it. You will just have to go, "I'm done. Goodbye, I'm done."

Finishing is beautiful. You never collect a check from a sales piece you don't finish.

Don't fall for the "Myth of Perfect," make it good enough and send it out.

4. FORCE YOURSELF TO GO FASTER

Actually, it's TWO hacks tied together.

1) Write as FAST as you can...

2) Write like you TALK

They both work together. If you force yourself to write quickly, you will write like you talk. And that's the key to great writing.

Again - if you want to write well, write fast. The faster you write, the better you write.

If you force yourself to write faster, you have to write the way you talk and it will force you to write simply.

It is no wonder our nation's laws are crammed to the gills with gobbledygook. They are written by people who can't put three understandable words together to save their lives.

Everybody wants to sound educated. No one wants to simply make sense.

Force yourself to write fast and the simple way you speak. It's extremely important to producing great copy because it gives your writing tremendous power.

5. SCHEDULE THE ENTIRE CAMPAIGN

Carefully think things through when you plan a marketing campaign... write down EVERYTHING that needs to happen. Put a date and an owner by each task. And then start knocking them off one by one.

For example, you need to identify the exact dates you want each piece to go out:

> January 17th - First Sales Letter
>
> January 31st - 2nd Sales Letter (to those who didn't buy)
>
> February 12th - 3rd Sales Letter (to non-buyers)

And so on... But there's more to add to that calendar... many business owners forget to include in their planning THE STEPS TO BUILD ALL THE PIECES IN THE CAMPAIGN! By that I mean, you need to also put in your plan:

> 1) A date to START writing letter 1, 2, 3
>
> 2) A date to FINISH letter 1, 2, 3
>
> 3) Dates to START/FINISH the associated website, etc. that's mentioned in the letter.
>
> 4) Dates to START/FINISH the phone/email script used when a lead calls in or emails you with questions.
>
> 5) Dates for Printing / Mailing / Etc. odds and ends associated with the project.

Bottom line - when you put together a campaign, it's more than "send a letter on DATE" - it's a complete project that you need to think through all the pieces involved.... which can and should include any necessary updates to your own business infrastructure.

6. USE SYSTEMS WHEN YOU WRITE

The real secret to fast, good, cheap is systematic thinking.

For example, let's take the very simple task of writing a sales letter to drum up some business with your target prospect. If you're one of those folks terrified of facing a blank page, then this is something that's going to concern you on all three angles.

-- It'll take a lot of time.
-- It'll cost buckets of money to hire out.
-- It's not likely to be very good.

Here's how having a system in place can help you overcome all three of these challenges:

1. Start building a swipe file of great sales letters. They don't need to be for your business - just start saving that junk mail that comes across your door.

2. When you see headlines that strike you as effective, write them down somewhere for use later on. I have pages and pages of different headlines that I save to kick-start my ideas.

3. Find a basic formula for the letter and stick to it. The easiest on the planet is PROBLEM-AGITATE-SOLVE. State the problem, twist the knife, and then show up for the rescue.

4. Write the first draft as fast as you can without stopping. Don't get fancy, don't try to impress with ten-dollar words, just write it out just as if you're talking to the customer directly.

5. Let the letter sit a day, come back and read it aloud, and fix anything that doesn't sound right.

6. Send it out and see what happens.

There you go. A quick, simple, and effective system for producing a sales letter that's fast, cheap, and good. It works because you're building upon a proven system.

CREATING KILLER OFFERS

(Hacks 7-17)

7. MAKE IT SO GOOD IT HURTS

The KEY to making sales in the EASIEST way possible boils down to a simple process that 99/100 business men and women FAIL to comprehend -

Make your offer sooooooooo incredibly good that it "hurts" when you lay it out for the prospect.

And when I say hurt, I mean HURT... as in it rips at your gut and you think you're a-gonna die.

All too often, the offer is kind of wishy-washy, unclear, and almost without a doubt sucking up to the business owner's best interests.

A great offer should really make YOU flinch, cringe, and weep just thinking about it.

Because that's what it takes to make it so awesome that resistance is futile.

Make it SO GOOD IT HURTS!

8. MAKE THEM IMAGINE THE JOY

Remember you're not selling the widget that you've stuck a price tag on – you're selling the RESULTS of buying that widget.

There's an old line about sales that goes, "people don't buy 1/8" drill bits – they're looking to create 1/8" inch holes."

So you begin with selling the result – but make sure you sprinkle in the mix the JOY that person will experience once they've got that result.

The word "imagine" can come in quite handy – as in "Imagine the sense of accomplishment and satisfaction you'll feel when you see all your hard work come together as you carry that brand new coffee table into your home. Imagine the smile on your wife's face as she carefully puts it into place in your family room."

You're pre-programming them to experience joy after experiencing the results of their decision to buy.

9. GIVE 'EM MORE THAN ONE OPTION

Too many business owners fall into the trap of just offering individual products/services for ONE price... which makes the sale pitch at the end basically "well, take it or leave it."

For example, when I was offering birthday party magic shows, I started off by just selling "the magic show."

The prospect had a YES or NO decision. That's it.

My marketing (and my business) got much better when I shifted from "the magic show" to offering multiple packages.

I took the easy route and created a SILVER Package and a GOLD Package – one at $197 and the other at $247.

This way you can word your sales close along the lines of "Well, those are my two packages, which sounds best to you?"

That way, it doesn't make this a "YES or NO" kind of decision, instead it's a choice between different options.

So always offer more than one option.

10. CREATE A SLACK ADJUSTER

When creating your suite of package options, toss in yet another package that's way off the charts in terms of its pricing.

For example, if you offer a $197 and $297 package, come up with one that's $697.

It's known in the trade as a "Slack Adjuster" and it serves several purposes:

1) It makes your other packages seem far more affordable in comparison. And in most cases, people will go for the one in the middle, because that's how we're wired.
2) There will be some people who will want your most expensive package. Maybe not a lot, but for sure some. And you very much want to have occasional big paydays along the way.

So come up with your "Slack Adjuster" deal as part of your package mix. It's a smart strategy and one well worth adding to your sales copy.

11. GET CREATIVE WITH YOUR GUARANTEE

Of course you should guarantee your products and services.

But don't just repeat something bland like, "money back guarantee."

Snazz it up a bit with a dash of creative flair by giving it a market-appropriate label.

For instance, for a magician, you might do something like:

- "The NOTHING UP MY SLEEVE!" guarantee!
- "NO SMOKE, NO MIRRORS, JUST RESULTS!" guarantee!
- "NO RABBITS IN THIS HAT, JUST THE MOST FUN EVENT YOU'VE EVER HAD OR IT'S FREE!" guarantee!

You get the idea. Get creative and obliterate one more objection your prospect may have for not pulling out their wallet.

12. WRITE YOUR OFFER FIRST

Before you brainstorm headlines, openings, transitions, closings, etc. nail down the totally KILLER offer you can make to your prospect.

In bullet point form, start by writing down every conceivable benefit of your offer.

Again, always remember to put yourself in your prospect's shoes. What are they looking for? What do they desire? What is it that they really, really want?

List every benefit of your product/service that you think they will accept and recognize as being a perfect fit for the needs, wants and desires they have.

Some writing experts say you should even go so far as create the exact order form for the program. That's not a bad idea and worth considering as well.

By creating your killer offer FIRST, you have a clear target towards which every single word of your sales copy can then point. From the opening headline to the final close, you know exactly where you plan to take them.

Try this out the next time you put together a sales letter, phone script, or website.

13. USE THE OFFER EQUATION

I've always loved puzzles, secret codes, cryptograms, and many other kinds of mental gymnastics. Of course, solving the puzzle of marketing is one of my great joys today - and here's an equation I learned from watching a presentation by the CEO of F5 Networks to a computer event on Cloud Computing (I am such a nerd...):

$$OFFER = CORE\ PRODUCT + VALUE\ ADD$$

Where:

OFFER -> that's what you sell, and to close the deal it had better be great.

CORE PRODUCT -> This is your basic service, which for a magician could be birthday party magic, balloon twisting, motivational school show, etc.

VALUE ADD -> ahhh.... here's the rub... this is that wonderfully unique thing that you and you alone bring to the table.

All too often we drop this last piece from our offers and instead rely on the Core Product as the key to making the sale. Big mistake. Because, as F5's CEO pointed out, Core Products - regardless of industry, be they high-tech or entertainment – eventually wind up becoming commodities... which means the only point of differentiation for the customer boils down to price.

When you ignore the critical element of "value add" when creating your offer, you get lumped into the mass category of everyone else doing that core product/service.

So your assignment is this: Nail down what it is about you and your product/service that provides that extra special "value add"?

Maybe it's that you provide it FASTER than anyone else. Maybe it's BIGGER than anything on the market. Maybe it relates to the book you wrote on the topic.

Whatever it is, you must add value that takes what it is you do/sell above and beyond just another commodity.

14. ASK THESE 5 QUICK QUESTIONS ABOUT YOUR OFFER

Here's a great tip from Yanik Silver. He's an amazing copywriter and he offered these FIVE QUICK QUESTIONS to ask yourself when thinking about your offer from the perspective of your prospect.

- Why ME?
- Why YOU?
- Why THIS?
- Why THIS MUCH?
- Why NOW?

Killer huh? Five simple, quick queries, but they nail down some core objections right from the get go.

Why ME? -- why does this offer matter to me?

Why YOU? -- what is it about YOU that makes this offer so special? Why should I listen to you?

Why THIS? -- tell me exactly why THIS specific offer / product / service is something I should care about.

Why THIS MUCH? -- just how do you justify the pricing? Why is it so much? OR... why is it so inexpensive?

Why NOW? -- give me a clear reason why I need to act right now to make that purchase decision.

Five quick questions that are all critically important to writing great sales copy.

Keep 'em in mind next time you put pen to paper.

15. PUMP UP YOUR GUARANTEE

Do you even have a guarantee for your products/services?

Listen, we live in an extremely skeptical age. People have lost trust in just about every institution you can imagine. Now, more than ever, you need to back up your services with a honkin' great guarantee.

Here a few ideas to consider when putting together your own guarantee:

- Make your guarantee dramatic and exciting. Give it a fun and interesting name, like "My No-Brainer, No Way You Lose, I'll Eat My Top Hat and Tear Up Your Check If You're Not Totally Satisfied Guarantee"
- Give your guarantee a value if possible. Identify what it's worth to the customer in believable terms.
- Try using multiple guarantees... for a magician example, not only will you guarantee the performance, you'll also guarantee that after you're done, every kid in the room will stand up and yell, "YAY MOM!"
- Create a Plus guarantee - you'll give them their money back plus something else, say a free show for their best friend!
- Finally, mention your guarantee a lot. Make sure they know you have so much faith in your services that they can be certain there's absolutely ZERO risk to them.

Crafting a great guarantee is just one more piece to your overall marketing message. But don't neglect it. It's a powerful persuasion tool.

16. GIVE YOUR OFFER URGENCY AND EXPLAIN WHY

Another method for generating immediate response is to give your offer a sense of urgency. Most businesses do this by writing something like, "Our calendar is filling up quickly!"

The problem is that everyone's saying that and I'm not sure prospects buy it.

A better method is to explain the reasons that they should take immediate action right away. You can do this by saying, "I'm fortunate enough to average 30 service calls a month so dates and times are limited. To avoid being disappointed, please call me right now at ...."

This is a truthful statement and it accomplishes a couple of things. First, it implies by the quantity of business that you do, you're in great demand and therefore, you must be good. Secondly, it plays upon the prospect's fear of loss.

Here's something motivational speaker Anthony Robbins said:

"People will do more to avoid the pain of loss than they will to gain pleasure*

17. HOW TO KNOW YOU HAVE A KILLER OFFER

The motivation for this comes from the total flameout of infrastructure I once had to face:

- The electricity in about half of my home went totally out - including my home office, which made working from home really fun. And even more fun...

- The power going out shut off my septic system pump, which meant my back yard was beginning to gurgle in unseemly ways.

- Even after fixing the electric, the breakers for the pump kept going out - which meant the septic pump needed replacing. NOW.

- So I called someone and got a new pump.

Here's the marketing lesson: I knew I needed a NEW Septic Pump. There wasn't any dithering or ifs/ands/buts. I needed a NEW Septic Pump. Had to have one. No questions asked. And I was going to get one.

And THAT is the kind of problem you want your offer to solve. Something THAT important in the mind of the prospect. Something that hits 'em right 'tween the eyes with "I GOTTA HAVE THAT!"

So when you craft your next offer, picture a backyard going sour because the septic system has failed... and YOU have the solution....

...Is YOUR solution that POWERFUL?

Someone out there's got a broken septic pump that YOU can fix. They NEED it fixed NOW.

You have the skills and the wherewithal to make things right. Go forth and make someone's life better.

HOW TO GET INSIDE YOUR CUSTOMER'S SKIN

(Hacks 18-23)

18. NAIL YOUR IDEAL CLIENT

You must spend the time to nail down the ideal client for the product/service you have to offer.

Too many words get wasted on generic "prospects" who don't exist.

If you're tasked with writing sales copy for yourself or a client and you do NOT understand them well enough to imagine sitting down across the table and having a real conversation – STOP the presses.

Before you start writing any kind of sales piece, you need to have a deep understanding of your target customer. Here's a series of questions you can use when identifying the exact person you're trying to target with your marketing message.

NOTE: Getting answers to these questions can also help you in defining and narrowing any list you might rent from a list broker.

19. ASK DEMOGRAPHIC QUESTIONS

Demographic questions tend to be superficial and/or obvious - but they definitely need to get asked:

- Gender - is there any kind of gender preference as it relates to your offer?
- How old is he/she?
- Married? Divorced? Single?
- Do they have kids? If so, what ages?
- Where do they live?

TIP: Go deeper and consider how they feel about these answers. For instance:

- How does he/she feel about being that age?
- How do you think they feel about parenting right now?
- Are they happy where they live or would they rather live somewhere else?

20. ASK ECONOMIC/LIFESTYLE QUESTIONS

Think through your perfect customer's relationship with money. And as with Demographics, ask the follow up question on how they FEEL about their current financial situation.

- What's their income range?
- What kinds of work do he/she do?
- If you're targeting a couple, do both work?

Another great question to think through and write out:

- What is their typical workday like - morning, workday, lunch, breaks, afternoon, drive home...?

21. ASK PSYCHOGRAPHIC QUESTIONS

Really get inside their heads to figure out what makes them tick. When you can answer these questions, you're able to identify the types of language and phrases they use to interact with their friends and peers. You want to sound like an old pal in your letter – these questions will provide you the ammo to do so.

- What websites do they visit? Social media do they use? How often? Do they visit blog sites... which ones? And do they post comments?
- What TV and Radio do they watch and listen to? When? How much? What kinds of programs - news and commentary? Home & Garden? Popular Culture/Hit Shows? Music?
- Where do they hang out when they're relaxing? Do they attend church? Sports events? Clubs & Associations? Do they like to eat out? Where? How often? How do they spend their weekends and free time?
- Are they political? Liberal? Moderate? Conservative? Concerned about politics or just oblivious? Do they vote every election or do they feel it's not worth their time?
- What does he/she read? Books? Magazines? Newspapers? How do they use the internet?

22. ASK THE "HEART-FELT" QUESTIONS

These questions require you to put on their moccasins and trudge a few miles down the dusty path with them. You want to know what gnaws at their stomach every waking moment.

- What keeps them awake at night?
    - How do they deal with these fears?
    - What do they hope for to solve their problems?
- What causes them pain right now?
- How much does it hurt?
    - How far would they go to get rid of it?
- What do they hope for?
    - What kinds of dreams do they have?
- Or have they given up?
    - Are they on the verge of despair or are they positive and looking ahead?

23. WRITE A LETTER FROM YOUR CUSTOMER ASKING YOU FOR HELP

I credit my friend Dave Dee with this idea, which I think is brilliant.

Sit down and write a letter from your customer asking for you to help them with the problem you and only you can solve.

Really get inside their head.

Feel what they feel.

Speak how they would speak.

This doesn't have to be a long letter, just enough so you can tell you "get" where they're coming from in regards to what you have to offer.

Imagine... if you spent even five minutes going through this process to visualize the person you're writing that sales letter for...

Wouldn't you have a much better chance of getting inside their head and their heart in conveying how much you can do for them?

Think about it.

FINE-TUNING YOUR LIST OF PROSPECTS

(Hacks 24-31)

24. MAKE SURE YOU REALLY KNOW YOUR LIST

The #1 factor to your success in direct mail is THE LIST that you mail to.

You cannot simply send out mailings scattershot and hope to get any kind of reasonable success.

The foundational key here is understanding your customer... what they want, need, fear, hope for, dream about... who they consider to be their enemy... what matters to them most...

When you have all that nailed down, you can start doing the leg work of picking out a list of prospective customers.

So... have you answered all the questions I listed earlier (and a few more of your own besides)?

If not, get busy.

25. WHO IS THEIR ENEMY?

When you can, you always want to sell against an enemy and make your prospects mad!

This is extremely powerful - it boils down to really knowing your prospect and who / what they consider to be one of the forces arrayed against them.

So...

Who is Your Perfect Client's ENEMY?

You may notice this used in an especially painful manner during any political season. Negative Political Ads are a great example of this tactic... and they can be oh-so effective.

Product / service companies often sell against their competition - either naming them directly or in other cases slyly referring them to "bargain brands" or "cheap knockoffs."

You don't HAVE to make your competitors the enemy – in fact, it's probably a mistake for many service businesses. There's plenty of business out there for all of us - and you simply can't do EVERY job, there is a limit to how much you can do at once.

The enemies you can sell against are options other than your service – for instance, if you're a CPA doing taxes you could sell against online tax tools, big name faceless corporations, or the pain of doing it yourself.

Whatever your market, there are options that you can clearly position yourself against as a clear and much preferable alternative.

Finally, don't miss out on the enemies of "hassle," "expense," and simply "doing nothing... which provides nothing." Sell against them hard in your materials as well.

26. CAN THEY AFFORD YOU?

Critical question to ask - can they afford to buy what you have to offer?

Hugely important.

Dan Kennedy tells the tale of a carpet cleaner who was going crazy over the fact his sales letters failed time and again to produce results. Dan was curious as the copy seemed solid, so they took a drive out to the neighborhoods where the letters were going.

They drove by house after house with cars up on blocks, litter everywhere, and guys on ramshackle porches drinking beer in torn t-shirts.

Kennedy noted, "So, do these guys look like having a clean carpet is a priority?"

Not quite. The list of these homes wasn't anything close to a reasonable match for the program being offered.

Make sure your target prospect has the ability to step up to your offer.

27. CAN YOU REACH THEM?

When choosing a market for your products and services, you need to ask this question before writing a single word:

Can they be reached in sufficient numbers?

Are you trying to reach someone who basically is unfindable?

Nowadays, with the disappearance of privacy, you can buy lists you can "select" down to a VERY specific group... GOP leaning Astrologists who subscribe to "HGTV" magazine and own a boat... maybe not that exactly, but awful darned close. But you need to make sure that you CAN target the folks you want.

NOTE: This has a related factor with doing SEO and Pay-Per-Click ads... is anyone out there really doing searches on the key terms you're thinking about using? Great question to ask.

28. CAN YOU RELATE TO THEM?

This is a BIGGIE... let's say you've nailed everything and you may have a target market that

a) has enough cash and

b) is easy to find and mail to.

Superb. But you still must be able to find a way <u>to relate to them</u>.

You must be able to connect through your messaging - that's critical to making any kind of direct mail campaign work. Maybe you simply pretend you can relate... if you can fake it, that's better than nothing.

But best of all is when you have a real affinity and affection for the people you're writing to and presenting your offer to...

That's why selling to magicians was so easy for me.

I've performed magic for decades now... I grew up around magic, gone to magic shops forever, and have performed (for money) forever.

I get what it's like to love magic and be a magician.

If I didn't, and I thought it was all crap, my feelings would come through...maybe not immediately, but sure enough given time you'd catch on there was something not quite right here...

You need to care about the people on your list.

If you can't, wrong list.

29. ANALYZE YOUR RESULTS

Dan Kennedy says repeatedly the unspoken copywriting secret to successful direct mail is the list itself. Great copy matters. Great lists matter as much, if not MORE.

When you do YOUR direct mail efforts, and look at the results, think about these kinds of factors.

1) What's the size of the campaign? Is this 1% out of 100? 1000? 10000? That's a key factor as you need an adequate sampling size for solid data.

2) Exactly how perfectly matched the offer was to the actual constituents on the list? For example, I'm still on an email list for pilots based on a project I worked on years ago. I'm not a pilot so offers specific to pilots aren't compelling to me these days, regardless of how well targeted or written.

3) Is the list compiled (i.e., they rounded up the names from public sources) or is it built from direct involvement with the publication? (i.e., subscribers)

4) Were these leads "hot" (i.e., had they purchased recently) or "cold" – they hadn't shown any activity in quite some time. (e.g., were they even still subscribers?)

5) What kind of postage was used? First class? Bulk rate? That could definitely be a factor.

30. DRILL DOWN ON YOUR LIST

One of the terms I learned while working at Microsoft was a phrase entitled "Drill Down." What it means is to move beyond a superficial analysis of some topic, problem, or idea and really think it through in detail. This is an extremely powerful concept. And it's one that you can and should apply to your marketing.

Here's a real example, which came to me while I was doing some work with an events company who had hired me to help them plan and market a software conference on the topic of "Cloud Computing." Part of my job was to figure out how to get attendees in the door.

Well, one set of attendees we want is what we've labeled thus far as *Software Developers* - you know, folks who write programs. I took some time to "drill down" a bit more on exactly who this "software developer" person is. And in putting that time, I realized that there were actually three types of folks to consider:

1. *Software Developers* who work on Cloud Computing software / services that get sold to businesses.

2. *Software Developers* who take Cloud Computing software / services and re-configure it for their specific industry and business - health care for instance.

3. *Software Developers* who work in corporate IT departments who have to make existing business applications properly communicate with new Cloud Computing applications being purchased by their companies.

So that generic *"Software Developer"* is actually a list of three VERY different individuals, each with very different hopes, dreams, fears, and pain when it comes to the topic of Cloud Computing.

Had I NOT done this analysis, I would have never really considered these differences. But once I did, it absolutely affected all the different elements of the marketing campaign and messaging as we reached out to these different groups.

When you create your sales copy, and as you identify all the many elements of your campaign - you need to really dive deep into what it is that makes the person who drives the buying decision tick.

31. AIM AT A SMALLER TARGET

Most business owners don't spend enough time selecting who they are going to market to. Not only do you have to select the right target market but you need to make sure that its size is manageable.

Most people think about how they can reach more and more people instead of how they can reach the most qualified people repetitively.

The key to your success is shrinking the size of your target market so you can market to them over and over again.

It is immeasurably better to contact a prospect list of 1,000 people continuously than it is to mail to 10,000 one-time.

That is why I love lead generation advertising. You can mail one, two, or three times (planting the farm) to a huge group of prospects and then only contact (email, call, etc.) those people who raise their hand and show that they are interested.

- If you have an extremely small target market, you should probably forgo lead generation and just start contacting them at least once a month.

- If you have a huge list of suspects, then you should absolutely use lead generation advertising in order to shrink the size of your target market.

Bottom line: You need to shrink the size of your TARGET market so you can contact your prospects repetitively.

HEADLINE HACKS

(Hacks 32-48)

32. MODEL HEADLINES FROM MAGAZINE COVERS

Keep your eyes peeled when looking over magazine covers.

I once noticed a magazine that my son-in-law Dave subscribes to. It's not one I typically read, as I'm not much of a hunting/fishing kind of guy...

"Outdoor Life"

Now it's wise to keep your mind open to new things, so rather than focus on learning about ammo, my mind snapped immediately to the headlines on the front cover. Here's a few:

"10 Tips to Help You Shoot Like a Sniper"

"The Ultimate Guide to Fishing the Great Lakes"

"Hot Tactics To Dupe Giant Walleyes"

"First Look: 12 Awesome New Hunting Boots"

"How to Pick the Perfect Arrow"

"Spot Clues that Say "Fish Here"

I loved these headlines so much, for a moment I thought about ripping the cover off but instead just snapped a photo with my phone.

Any one of these could be turned into a killer headline or subhead in a sales letter or website for your business. For instance, a Wedding Planner could offer a free report:

"The Ultimate Guide to Planning the Most Incredible Wedding Reception Ever!"

An Information Technology Consultant could relay:

"10 Hot Tips to Help You Launch Your Next Successful Product"

A local CPA could offer:

"How to Pick the Perfect Strategy to Reduce Your Taxes in 2017"

Get the idea? Just because the headline was originally purposed for guns/ammo/fish/game doesn't mean it can't be re-written and repurposed to promote your biz.

Some of the most talented copywriters on the planet come up with those headlines - and they'll pay off for you as well!

33. QUICK AND DIRTY HEADLINE TEMPLATES

I hate to reinvent the wheel... that's why I love templates and swipe copy. Here are some cool headline starters for your next sales piece:

\-

Give me _____ and I'll _____ Ways to _____

Dare to try our _____ and discover the secret to _____

If you are _____, you can _____

What You Should Know About _____

When Experts _____, This is what they do....

Little Known Ways to _____ and What it Takes to _____

\-

Let me give you a great little tip:

Combine these snippets to create longer headlines. Don't lock yourself into single sentence / short headlines... a great headline can run on for as many words as it needs to grab 'em by the throat and make 'em pay attention.

Dan Kennedy says that your headline should be so good it could stand alone as a classified ad with a phone number / web address beneath it.

That's something to shoot for.

34. ROCK STAR WORDS FOR HEADLINES

A great headline is CRITICAL to making your sales letters and sales pieces work. If you can't draw them in with a powerful headline, your chance of getting them to read further into the copy fades away.

One of the keys to killer headlines is to use language and words that connect on a subconscious, emotional level. You don't want to try to "logically" persuade with your headline - you want to GRAB 'EM!

Here are some kick-butt words to plant in your headlines:

Advice to....

Announcing:

At Last...

Finally...

Secrets of...

New

Powerful

How to...

Proven...

Then, the 3 mega-rock star words of headline-dom:

FREE

You

Your

Use 'em and close some deals.

35. HEADLINE HACK QUESTION – YOUR NAME?

Quick question: Does your headline rely primarily on the power of your NAME alone?

E.g., "Hire Bonzo the Magnificent for Your Party!"

This is not a good strategy. Unless you're Madonna, your name as a headline is a "dead line."

36. HEADLINE HACK QUESTION - WHO?

Does your headline speak to a specific person you've carefully chosen?

You should write ALL your copy with a very clear target in mind.

Even your headline should reflect the fact that your services are aimed at them and their wants, needs, fears, and pain – and not the entire world.

37. HEADLINE HACK QUESTION - BOLD CLAIM?

Does your headline make a bold claim with powerful benefits?

Don't be shy about proclaiming the value of your service to that person you've identified.

Instead, shout it from the rooftops!

And make sure your reader can tell instantly why that headline matters to them.

38. HEADLINE HACK QUESTION - INTERESTING?

Is your headline interesting?

No one wants to read any more boring blah-de-blah-de-blah ad copy.

In fact, no one wants to read anything. Especially same old same old boring.

Your headline has to grab me by the throat in order to keep my attention and make me want to learn more.

39. HEADLINE HACK QUESTION - CONFUSING?

Is your headline confusing?

Can you look at it and instantly understand what it's all about? Or is it "clever" and you have to think it through to figure it out.

Worse than boring is confusing... your headline has to be clear in what it promises to deliver.

40. HEADLINE HACK QUESTION - CLASSIFIED AD?

Could your headline stand alone as a classified ad?

This is a great test. The best headlines can stand all by themselves as a classified ad. Just the headline, nothing else, and it would still pull in leads.

41. USE THIS EMOTIONAL HEADLINE TOOL

Here's a very fun little headline evaluation tool you can use to plug in your headlines for their "Emotional Marketing Value."

You gotta grab 'em by the throat and yank tight the heartstrings when writing copy these days.

And crafting a powerful headline is job one in making that happen. I can't vouch 1000% for the accuracy of this little rascal, but it is fun to play with and certainly worth a quick look-see when crafting your next headline:

http://www.aminstitute.com/headline/

Check it out and have some fun.

42. 7 MORE EASY HEADLINE FORMULAS

Here are 7 More Easy formulas for creating your own benefit-driven headline. Fill in the blanks with the results you know your customers will want to achieve.

How To _____

Discover Why _____

The Secret To _____

Who Else Wants _____

The 7 Reasons _____

Important News For _____

Everywhere _____ Are Raving About _____

For example,

"Who Else Wants to Have a Company Picnic That Every Employee and Their Families Will Rave About For Years To Come!?"

Or...

"Important News for PTA Presidents Who Want To Know The Easiest Way To Raise Money For Their School Without Spending a Dime Or Having to Sell Tons of Candy, Sweets, or Books!"

Find out what your prospects want and give it to them right between the eyes with a powerful, attention grabbing headline.

43. ADD SELF-INTEREST TO EVERY HEADLINE

Here's a piece of great advice from marketing legend John Caples on creating that oh-so-critical element of every sales letter – the headline:

"First and foremost, try to get self-interest into every headline you write. Make your headline suggest to the reader that here is something he wants."

For example, you'll all too often see headlines like this:

Jack Jones Chevrolet – In Business Since 1948!

Where's the self-interest? Totally lacking.

Instead, for that same car dealership, how about this:

The One Dealership in Northwest Kentucky Dedicated to Making Owning Your Next Car Fast, Simple, and Always Affordable – Since 1948!

Remember, your headline (as well as the rest of your ad copy) has to be more about THEM and not you.

44. FOLLOW THESE 9 SIMPLE RULES FOR HEADLINES

Here are some guidelines to effective headlines well worth salting away for future reference:

1. Make it BIG and BOLD. The bigger and bolder the better.

2. Do NOT USE ALL CAPS FOR THE ENTIRE HEADLINE. It makes it difficult to read. Capitalizing the first letter of every word has been proven to be effective.

3. "Quotation marks around the headline" have been shown to increase response.

4. Both long and short headlines work well as long as they "speak" to your prospect's interest.

5. Write headlines in a National Enquirer style. If you don't agree, tell me with a straight face that your head doesn't snap left to the tabloids every time you buy groceries. They are EXPERTS at grabbing attention. You need to be too.

6. Don't be cute or try to be clever. If your prospect has to guess what your advertisement or letter is about after they read your headline, it sucks and you lose.

7. Don't talk about how great you are. Speak to your prospect's interests and desires.

8. Don't try to "trick" your prospect into reading your ad or letter. "FREE SEX!" as a headline will certainly get attention but you're just going to anger your prospect when they continue reading and find out that you are trying to sell them a magic show.

9. Do NOT send out or hand out any piece of printed material that does not have a headline. Ever.

Nine simple rules that will serve you well.

45. USE THE RIGHT WORDS IN HEADLINES

Make sure your copy leverages the 10 top money making words you should use in your headlines. John Caples, who was head of the third largest ad agency in the US for 40 years, analyzed the most commonly used words in 100 successful headlines. Here's what he found:

You... used 31 times

Your... 14 times

How... 12 times

New... 10 times

Who.... 8 times

Money.. 6 times

Now.... 4 times

People..4 times

Want....4 times

Why.....4 times

The most common words ... of course... were "you" and "your". It should be obvious. When you're writing to sell, the biggest mistake most often made is to focus on "We" and "I". Look through the valpack ads you get in the mail. How many times do you see ads that only tell "our story"? Do you care? Me neither.

Using the right words is critical to making salesletters do the job.

46. USE ONE OF THESE THREE EASY HEADLINE STARTERS

Still stuck? Get simple and try one on these three easy headline starters:

1. The Secret of....

2. How to.....

3. Who Else...

Just add your own customer benefit to the starter. For instance,

"The Secret of Having a Birthday Party Your Child Will Never Forget and Treasure Forever!"

or

"How to Make Your Next Holiday Party the Most Unforgettable Experience Your Company Has Ever Had!"

Get the idea? Use the power of these easy headline starters to jump-start your next marketing message.

47. WRITE ONLY HEADLINES AND SUBHEADS FIRST

Start with your headlines and subheads. Create these first before writing any copy.

Create the entire sales piece with just these. Then fill in the blanks with real copy.

The headlines and subheads are key what's known as the dual-readership path.

Some people skim and read only headlines and subheads.

Some read word for word, top to bottom, start to finish.

When you focus on Headlines and Subheads first, it enables you to make sure what you're saying communicates effectively to both styles – someone can just skim your letter and get very quickly to your message.

48. CONSCIOUSLY DESIGN HOW LINES BREAK

This is something I learned from Dan Kennedy – a very cool tip that as I recall he barely gave any time or mention to.

As the copywriter, YOU are responsible for the look of your copy. If you have a headline that shows up like this:

The One Dealership in Northwest Kentucky Dedicated to Making Owning Your Next Car Fast, Simple, and Always Affordable – Since 1948!

That's not bad, but it could be better – put in line breaks at the key points you want the reader to focus on. For instance:

The One Dealership in Northwest Kentucky
Dedicated to Making Owning Your Next Car
Fast, Simple, and Always Affordable – Since 1948!

Get the difference? It's more art than science, but it can bring the message home much more effectively when used properly.

WRITING HACKS

(Hacks 49-98)

49. USE THE 10 REASONS ANYONE BUYS ANYTHING

I came across a very interesting data point in one of my swipe file documents. It's entitled *"Top 10 Reasons Anyone Buys Anything."* Now, in the interest of full disclosure, the expert listing these doesn't state his sources, so this could well be total fluff... however, I think not as these have a solid feel in my opinion. So here you go:

1. Make money.
2. Save money.
3. Save time.
4. Avoid effort.
5. Increase comfort.
6. Achieve greater cleanliness.
7. Obtain fuller health.
8. Escape physical pain.
9. Claim praise.
10. Be popular.

Sound pretty reasonable to me, howzabout you?

Yeah. Thought so.

So in writing your next piece of lead-generation or sales copy, how many of these hot buttons do you think you can blend into the mix? If you're a magician creating a new website for birthday moms for instance, I'd say you could at least involve:

- Saving money: you are totally affordable!
- Avoiding effort: it will be soooooo easy!
- Increasing comfort: you can just relax....
- Escape physical pain: no crying, unhappy kids - aggh!!!
- Claim praise: Every other mom will go wow!!!!
- Be popular: Your child will LOVE you!

Looks like these 10 hot buttons can definitely help out in defining some benefits for your programs.

Give them a shot.

50. THE WORLD'S SIMPLEST SALES LETTER FORMULA

Here's the world's SIMPLEST Sales Letter Formula for you to take and use the next time you want to crank out copy for your website, a direct mail piece, or just about any other piece that's intended to CLOSE-the-DEAL.

It's good for any market and just about any media.

1. Use a bold, compelling, benefit-oriented headline at the top of the letter.
2. In your introduction, use a lot of benefit-oriented bullet points.
3. Make your KILLER offer... describe it in terms of the TRANSFORMATION the customer will experience when they make the deal.
4. Give your offer a HARD deadline.
5. Have a clear, specific call to action. Don't futz around, ASK FOR THE SALE and tell them exactly what to do.
6. Summarize your offer in the first P.S.
7. Repeat your call to action in the PPS.

Once you get these points down, then flesh it out with a little personality, sub-heads that answer key objections, some social proof (i.e., testimonials and your credentials), and toss in a "you can't lose!" guarantee.

Very simple, straightforward and yet... POWERFUL.

51. NAIL DOWN THE TRANSFORMATION

I'm going to reveal a core copy principle that I gleaned from experience and from the pages of a classic book on magic – Dariel Fitzkee's "Trick Brain." ...

It's something that I've seen totally forgotten when reviewing websites, sales letters, and other types of copy from all kinds of businesses. And it boils down to this question:

"What is the KEY Transformation that will occur as a result of your product or your service?"

This is SO important.

People don't care what you do or what you sell, they care only about the results you've delivered in relation to the problem they needed solved... and life should be BETTER in a clear cut way after you've finished.

So what is the TRANSFORMATION your product/service delivers?

It should be significant and meaningful.

If not, why are you even bothering to offer it?

Whatever it is you deliver, make sure to lay it out in crystal clear terms of a "before-and-after" kind of transformation.

This is essential to writing great copy that sells.

52. GET FOCUSED BY WRITING IT AS A CLASSIFIED AD

A great classified ad is short, focused, and delivers results. How does it do this? By focusing on the basics that every sales piece must nail to succeed.

- Identifies who your ideal prospect is and, by inference, who you don't want to respond.
- Presents a powerful, benefit-oriented headline.
- Teases the prospect so he or she wants to learn more.
- Makes a specific, easy non-threatening call to action.

Here's an example of a lead generation ad from a magician targeting Meeting Planners who might be interested in an entertainment program:

****

Attention Meeting Planners...

Make Your Next Meeting Impressive & Unforgettable With Unique Programs Of Mindreading, Magic & Hypnosis. Call 1-800-555-5555, 24 Hours, For A Free Recorded Message To Get Your FREE Information Package That Will Show You How To Make Your Next Meeting The Best Ever. There's no obligation. Call Today!

****

Simple. Direct. Clear from start to finish.

If you're stuck, try writing it first as a classified ad to focus your thinking and make sure you truly know what you want to achieve.

53. MODEL BLACK FRIDAY'S BEST

Here's why I LOVE Black Friday:

1> It's your chance to experience madness, chaos, and mayhem with your significant other as you explore the wonders of capitalism.
2> You can do your part to make the economy stronger by dropping some change on gifts for the upcoming Christmas holiday.

But the biggest reason I love Black Friday:

3> You can see how REALLY smart copywriters and marketers promote products & services!

You betcha, it's a veritable feeding frenzy for ever-hungry marketing sharks like you and me to gorge ourselves upon. Forget the turkey, hand me the junk mail and newspaper inserts!

Now there's where you'll find some tasty treats to like headlines to re-purpose, envelope copy to swipe, and outrageous advertising to model.

Enjoy your holiday with family and friends and keep a sharp eye out for great marketing you can learn from.

54. USE TESTIMONIALS TO BACK UP CLAIMS

Of course you need to use testimonials – in fact, if possible EVERYTHING you send out as a sales piece should have some testimonials and/or social proof built-in.

Just adding testimonials gives you additional street cred with your prospect. Here are a few quick thoughts on their use:

- Text is good. Audio is better. Video is best.
- Offer a transcribed version of an audio or video testimonial as well.
- With text, adding a picture of the person giving the testimonial adds credibility.
- Use the full name, not single letters ala "J. says..."
- Include the hometown and state if you can.
- NEVER make up testimonials. Just not worth it.
- When making a point about a benefit, follow it with a testimonial that backs up that point (really powerful).

55. DON'T BE BORING

When you ask your teenaged son or daughter whether they're interested in hanging out with you to check out a classic old black-and-white film you've loved for years... maybe one that stars top-tier stars from the glamorous days of Hollywood's Golden Era... the one word answer you're likely to get is this:

BORING!!!!

Nevertheless, there's a painful marketing reality exposed by this response - a reality that we all as marketers need to acknowledge.

You can't be BORING!

Sales letters, postcards, Facebook posts, emails, billboards, radio, whatever... the cardinal sin for all marketing is to blend in with the tedious, echoing blather that fills the mailboxes and airwaves with same-old, same-old content.

All the sales copy you write (or have written) needs to express the powerful benefits of your programs and your offers in ways that stand out from the crowd.

As Dan Kennedy put it, one reason he's so successful as a writer is that he "says interesting things in interesting ways."

Resolve from this point forward to make all of your marketing BOLD, Creative, and relentlessly i-n-t-e-r-e-s-t-i-n-g.

56. ASK THESE FOUR QUESTIONS

I love great headlines and subject lines, which is why I wanted to share this from the very sharp pencil of famed copywriter Maxwell Sackheim.

When evaluating copy, he offered these 4 guidelines:

1 – Why should anyone read or listen to it?

2- Why should anyone believe it?

3 – Why should anyone do anything about it?

4 – Why should it be acted up immediately?

Those are four, tough, good questions to ask every time you prepare an ad, letter, brochure, and postcard.

The first should be answered due to the fact you took some time and carefully chose a specific target market... And then aimed your offer to hit them right between the eyes.

But even with the audience properly nailed, you still need to answer the other questions - the devil's in the details when it comes to closing the deal with your sales copy.

Having this kind of short cut working on your side makes great sense... and your writing job easier.

57. USE THE A-I-D-A FORMULA

In case you want something F-A-S-T when writing your promotional copy, here's a Classic 4-step copywriting formula that should be used really with ANY piece of copy you create. It goes like this:

A-I-D-A

- Attention
- Interest
- Desire
- Action

You need ALL four steps in every piece of copy.

- **Attention** - typically done by the headline, which must GRAB your prospect's attention by being so compelling they must keep reading.
- **Interest** - here's where you show that you "feel their pain"... you know what problem they need solved and you get how it feels to have that hanging over them.
- **Desire** - this is where you make your offer to SOLVE their problem - and hit 'em with both barrels in laying out all the bells and whistles of what you can do.
- **Action** - now don't wimp out... you MUST give CLEAR instructions on what they should do next, either call, click, email or buy...and NOW, it must be urgent.

A-I-D-A ... simple yet extremely effective and all four elements need to be in every bit of sales prose you create.

58. STOP TRYING TO CONVINCE THEM

I think this is an extremely important sales concept that FAR too many businesses fail to grasp.

It's based on a key point made by marketer Jeff Paul who's famed primarily for a direct response ad that turned his life totally around. Paul knew how to write great sales copy. But his key insight is something that you need to embrace:

"Convincing anyone of anything sucks."

The way you AVOID this reality boils down to two things:

1) Be so good your clients tell other people about you.
2) Choose prospects who are already in a place where what you offer is the perfect solution to what they need.

That 2nd thing is JUST as important as the first.

You CANNOT be all things to all people.

But you surely can be THE THING for a limited number of people.

Figure out who those people are - exactly what they want - and be the answer they're searching for.

Then you hardly have to sell at all.

59. APPLY THE ELMORE LEONARD PRINCIPLE

One of the world's great crime novelists was Elmore Leonard. He was the author of "Get Shorty" and a number of other massively successful books.

He offered 10 great principles on writing novels, but it's number 10 that applies 10000% to writing copy:

#10.... *"leave out the part that readers tend to skip."*

Even in copy, which can go on and on it may seem, you MUST edit to keep it tight and as concise as possible.

Every word counts in copy, just like in story-telling.

Every word must drive home the key point (i.e., key "selling" point) you want to make.

And every word must be compelling - again, the cardinal sin for marketing is to be BORING.

 Be ruthless in reviewing your copy to make sure you adhere to this principle.

60. PERSONALIZE THE COPY

Want to dramatically boost your response rate for your direct mail campaigns?

It's so simple...

Personalize your sales letters.

Look, most small businesses are doing small mailings of 100, 200, 300, 400, 500 pieces. (You can easily have this done even if you're mailing thousands of pieces as well.)

One of the best ways to personalize a letter is by <u>putting your prospect's name in the headline.</u>

There's no way you can ignore the headline when it's YOUR NAME there at the top.

Putting your prospect's name in the headline is going to catch their attention.

I encourage you to try it. Taking the extra time to get noticed is just one of the keys to your success.

61. MAKE 'EM MAD!

Like that guy down the street who you never suspected of going berserk, people would say:

"He was always such a quiet man..."

Quiet. Right. Like that kid Norman Bates.

Well, no one will mistake me for a "quiet man" - in fact, quite the opposite. Far too often I can't keep my big yap shut. Much to my chagrin and even despair.

I like to talk, hey, that's how it is. It's how I'm wired.

Well, one thing we're ALL wired to notice is when someone connects to us EMOTIONALLY.

Now that emotion may not always be positive - hence, "DON'T MAKE ME MAD!"

You bet, anger's a powerful emotion. And so's fear and pain.

And all three of those **Anger, Fear, and Pain are GIGANTIC keys to making your direct response marketing more effective.**

If you can hit a nerve in your reader's soul, you will be able to connect on a deep level - one that will let you in the door to showing that you ARE on their side.

Professional copywriters know that when using that old formula - Problem, Agitate, Solve - for a sales letter, the more AGITATION you can generate... twisting that knife until it really hurts... the better it will feel in the heart of the prospect when you deliver relief in terms of your most excellent product or service.

Work at connecting EMOTIONALLY with your marketing.

It's a hugely valuable tool to add to the arsenal.

62. NEVER START FROM A BLANK PAGE

This will save you acres of grief. Don't try to write that sales letter, web page, brochure, whatever while staring at a white piece of paper or a blank screen.

Grab something... anything... a piece of copy from your swipe file, a direct response ad from today's paper, a classified ad in a magazine, an old letter you wrote years back - ANYTHING... and start with that as your template.

Use it to generate the headline - something that will grab your customer's attention with a result and a benefit they will love.

Use it to create the overall outline of your sales piece... use the subheads and tweak them a bit to fit with your offer.

Just take something and make it into something different and new and fitting to you.

Never start from nothing... you will write so much faster if you start from something, anything and rework it to become yours.

That is a KILLER professional writing tip. Big time.

Use it the next time you feel stymied when writing.

63. ADD SOME ARRRRR TO YOUR USP

"Arrrrrr"

I'm not normally a huge fan of "branding" but I have to give the guys who came up with "Talk Like a Pirate Day" a great big thumbs up!

It's a wonderful lesson in developing a Unique Selling Proposition (aka USP). Out of all the days in the year, in the decade since they first were mentioned in a column by Dave Barry, this snazzy idea has caught on like wild-fire... it's gone global.

Of course, they have leveraged this fame with all kinds of "pirate-themed" swag and booty.

Very smart!

Here are three keys to "Arrrrrr"

1. It's got a clear hook. "Talk like a Pirate." Crap, how can you forget that!
2. It's FUN - come on, who doesn't enjoy doing a bad pirate accent!
3. It's interactive - everyone can get involved in one way or another... in fact, that's the core idea!

And I'll toss one more key that makes this so cool...

4. It links to CELEBRITY... this has really taken off with the Johnny Depp "Pirates of the Caribbean" series. They managed to ride the wave of piracy splendidly!

So... can you make your USP as powerful as this?

64. MAKE THE DAMAGING ADMISSION

This is more like a "pre-emptive strike" against the damage done when a prospect doesn't believe your offer. It's the copywriting principle known as the:

"Damaging Admission"

... and it's a really smart tool to use in your sales materials - letters, websites, brochures and even telephone scripts.

It's simple: Just state out front to the prospect what you would consider a weakness of your offer.

Reason: It's best to get this out in the open and identify a pro-active response to this potential objection before the prospect comes out with it on their own.

Example: Back when I was doing family magic shows, in my phone script I would lay out up front that as a magician, I didn't do the "artistic act with floating things synchronized to music" - so if you're looking for that kind of magic act, I'm not your guy.

I was being totally upfront about what could be considered a "weakness" in my act - I'm not a traditional "magician" with top hat, cane, and bunny. Not my shtick. Nothing against that sort of thing, it just wasn't me and never will be.

Instead, I let them know my focus was to create a room packed with howling, laughing kids. That's what I deliver.

So... my "damaging admission" led right into what was essentially my Unique Selling Proposition.

Might this turn off some prospects? Maybe. But you can't book every gig. I'm not right for everyone everywhere. That's fine.

This does, however, produce great results for me again and again as I'm hitting on the highest level of needs in most folks who call for that kind of show.

Look at your offer honestly and think about how you might turn something that's a possible drawback into a lead right into your strongest positive.

65. MASTER COPYWRITER HACK #1

What I have here is a really solid list for writing G-R-E-A-T copy from a guy is quite clearly one of the best in the biz: John Carlton. The numeric points are John's; me, I'll kibbutz from the sidelines below each.

Carlton: "Use POWER words. Humiliate. Assault."

Power words are interesting.

They imply action. Movement. Force. Confidence.

As Strunk & White said so well in "Elements of Style:"

>*"Make definite assertions!"*

Power words help you do so.

66. MASTER COPYWRITER HACK #2

Carlton: "Use Action verbs. No adjectives."

Use ACTIVE verbs, not passive... i.e., write in Active Voice "someone did something" not "something is being done by something."

And flowery adjectives clutter and gum up the prose.

Say what you want to say directly and to the point.

67. MASTER COPYWRITER HACK #3

Carlton: "Use storytelling verbs...imagine, dream..."

People LOVE stories.

Just stating the phrase, "Let me tell you a story about…" makes us automatically stop what we're doing to listen. We can't help ourselves. That's just how we're wired.

Any time you can find a way to bring even a hint of tale-telling into your copy do so.

68. MASTER COPYWRITER HACK #4

Carlton: The So What test. After every sentence think, "so what?"

This is a superb practice because it FORCES you to get into the mind of the customer and then consider their possible objections to what you write.

This leads to more quality thinking being applied to the benefits you THINK you're conveying.

For instance, just saying "winner of local magic competition!" ... well, so what?

The what is "which means you can be certain you're getting a guy who's proven he can deliver the goods and provide a quality performance as measured against other competitors."

69. MASTER COPYWRITER HACK #5

Carlton: "Get the rhythm of the copy by reading it out loud."

Strive to have your writing sound like the way you talk.

Writers call this "finding your voice." It takes real dedication and practice to get there, plus the knowledge that writing like you talk is a real goal.

You do NOT want to sound like an English Textbook.... bleah!

70. MASTER COPYWRITER HACK #6

Carlton: "Study great copywriting."

Where do you find great copy?

JUNK MAIL!

Especially the letters you've gotten over and over again.

If the copy worked well enough to get sent multiple times, then you know it's getting good results.

Read it. Save it. Rely on it. Learn from it.

71. MASTER COPYWRITER HACK #7

Carlton: "Great copywriting has a cadence to it - It's easy, it's fast, it'll change your life."

This resonates with the "write like you talk" rule. But without the stammering, ums, pauses, etc.

Good copy flows... and again, the best way to tell is to read it aloud.

72. MASTER COPYWRITER HACK #8

Carlton: "Use slang for the appropriate market. Talk like your market talks. Make sure you know the language of your prospects."

Once again, this PROVES to your prospect that you have taken the time to understand where they live and what they're going through.

Using their own language properly helps you build a connection... and that in turn helps you make that sale in print.

73. MAKE SURE _YOU_ COMES THROUGH

Here's a quick test of your copy and your sales materials... Look them over with as impartial an eye as humanly possible. Then ask yourself this question:

> "Does this look/sound/read like it's coming from a warm, living, breathing human being ... or like it was created by a faceless, cold, organization?"

Answer honestly.

This goes for ALL marketing - everything we use to promote ourselves has to SHINE through with PERSONALITY!

No-one wants to do business with a faceless corporate entity.

We want to share time and money with real people that we can relate to and feel like we could get to know.

Now... this does involve some risk... and the risk is that maybe some folks will not like the real you! When you expose yourself warts and all to the world, it's all too true that what you say, write, video, and do won't please everyone.

That was hard for me to accept. I'm the kind of guy who wants EVERYONE to love me.

But that's nonsense - no matter how big a sweetheart I am, there will be those for whatever foolish, short-sighted, sub-human instinctual throwback to knuckle-drag-dom will find that I rub 'em the wrong way.

Ho-kay. So it goes. Next.

That's a risk you and I both need to take when it comes to our marketing.

Again - check out your websites, your brochures, flyers, and everything else you send out or display - see if you in all your crazy, imperfect, unique and unforgettable glory comes through.

Because that's the real somebody your customer craves.

74. HAVE A CLEAR GOAL / CALL TO ACTION

Make sure you're clear on what it is you want your copy to accomplish, i.e., what do you want its reader to do after reading?

For a website, my goal is to get them to contact me. Period. I don't try to make the sale with the website.

For a letter, you CAN try to sell them OR you can just try to get them to make contact. Either is acceptable.

Not having a clear and simple goal for your copy is a huge mistake that many make.

Don't confuse your prospect. Make it 100% clear what you want them to do.

75. FILL YOUR COPY WITH POWER WORDS

You want to always strive to create an emotional connection with your copy. And one of the best ways to make your sales copy sing is to ditch boring, lackluster language and instead use words that have some oomph!

Here's a few to get you started:

- Colossal
- Enormous
- Breakthrough
- Boost
- Eye-Catching
- Five-Star
- Jam-Packed
- Jump on the Bandwagon
- Ironclad
- Pay Dirt
- Smart
- Skyrocket

That'll get you started, but there's plenty more to consider.

The key point here: don't settle for mundane when writing copy. Make sure what you write catches the eye and tickles the ear. Speak from the heart. Speak with passion. And sell at full bore and flat out.

76. BE BOLD

I love great sayings. I believe in not only collecting them, but also committing them to memory so you have them as a mental resource you can pull out and use at just the right time or situation.

Here's a great quote from marketing legend Dan Kennedy:

> "Most marketing messages are wimpy. They basically enlarge the business card. They say the same things everybody else is saying. They make vague, image building statements. They end without a call to action."

Go back to the marketing messages you have on your biz card, your website, your sales / promo letters and ask yourself: "**Am I being bold enough here?**"

If you have a great product/service, you have a DUTY to sell HARD - not only for your clients, but also for the good of your market. Don't allow crappy competitors to succeed just because they have the balls to promote themselves more powerfully than you.

Be bold. Make a strong statement. Ask for the sale.

You've worked hard and you deserve to be first in line.

77. HIT 'EM WHERE IT HURTS

This is about creating ads that get read. It applies to postcards, letters, display ads, but right here I'm going to cover how this works for Pay Per Click ads and the headlines you put on your website.

When you're building out your list of key words for your website and your Google Ads, the goal you have is to nail down as close as possible exactly what it is your prospect will type into Google before hitting ENTER.

In order to do this, it really requires that you understand your prospect in detail. Not just at a superficial level, you really need to get inside their heads and feel what's going on deep within as those gears grind away. The closer you can come to hitting that person in mid-thought, the better luck you'll have in getting the lead.

It's that "mid-thought" thing that gets you serious traction.

Here's a quick story that points out exactly how important that is.

One client I had does what's called "permanent cosmetics" - which is basically cosmetic tattoos, such as eyeliner, lips, etc. Of course, the key words she wanted were "permanent cosmetics" - which does get a lot of searches. And when I asked her to tell me what prospects typically wanted, she told me that she did a lot of business from folks who basically needed a badly done job repaired.

"Perfect" I said, "that's just what I needed to know." So we did a split test in her Adwords account.

One ad was the one she wanted, which was basically along the lines of

> Permanent Cosmetics
> Need help? Best in town.
> Contact:....

As a test, I gave her this one to put up against it:

Permanent Cosmetics
I'll fix the screw ups you got from
the bargain technician.

Guess which worked best? You got it. Number two blew the
doors off the other, more standard ad. And she's getting biz now
left and right from her Google Adwords account. She's thrilled.

The reason that ad works is that it hits the prospect right where
it hurts. They read it and weep. And then they click to learn
how to make that pain go away.

That's your job when writing your ads. Know the pain and
promise to make it go away. You can do this. All it takes is a
little work and a little empathy for that person you care deeply
about: Your customer.

78. USE THE MOST IMPORTANT WORD IN COPYWRITING

I'm going to reveal the single most important word you HAVE to include in all your website copy... And it's only three letters:

"YOU"

The most common copywriting mistake most often seen is the "I" word and its bosom buddies, "my" and "we".

"I have over 20 years of experience."

"I have been in business since 1996."

"We belong to the local Chamber of Commerce."

"My homemade pizza sauce was invented by our Great-grandma and I always use it for all family celebrations..."

Frankly, who cares? I don't. And I bet you don't either. It's sad but true - nobody really cares about you. Unless you're already a celebrity, your name doesn't mean squat to Joe or Jane Public.

They care about themselves and the problem they think you might be able to solve. Period.

So when you write, tell a story ... in your own words, just like you'd be sitting across the table, just me and you... that shows you understand where I'm coming from, you get the situation I'm facing and need help with, and you've successfully solved this kind of problem over and over and over again.

And you even have the photos, the audios, some video, and even signed letters to prove it.

Great. Now I'll listen to you. I might even be interested in hearing about your 20 years of experience. Maybe...

But skip all the "me me me" stuff and start singing a tune that matters to the customer.

You. You. You.

Three little letters that prove you have my best interests at heart.

Use 'em.

79. APPLY THE SIX WEAPONS OF INFLUENCE

A fantastic book on marketing... that really is not about marketing at all... is this one by Robert Cialdini: *"Influence: The Psychology of Persuasion"*

Based on copious research, Cialdini explains exactly how we are wired to respond to certain stimuli - and even if we know that wiring, we still can't help ourselves. Marketers and Salesmen use these principles ALL the time to push the buttons on their prospects.

Cialidini identifies SIX Key "Weapons of Influence"

- **Reciprocity** - People want to return a favor. This is why you get tons of free samples in marketing.
- **Commitment and Consistency** - When you commit to an idea or goal, you are more likely to honor that commitment no matter what to maintain your sense of self image.
- **Social Proof** - You will follow the crowd. If there's a bunch of buyers already, you want to join them and buy too.
- **Authority** - You can't help but respect the opinions of others who have authority.
- **Liking** - We all are more likely to be persuaded by someone we find likable. (This is a key principle IMO as a magician - you have to be likable!)
- **Scarcity** - Perceived scarcity - either in quantity or a time-limit - will generate demand.

These are wired into our human natures. Hence, there's real power in knowing these principles and using them in your marketing and sales materials.

Next time you're putting together a sales letter, or a proposal, or a new offer – brainstorm for a couple minutes to consider how you can apply one or more of these "Six Weapons" to what you're crafting.

80. APPLY THESE 4 WORDS TO EVERYTHING YOU WRITE

This is perfect for anyone getting ready to put some finishing touches on a website, sales letter, brochure, business card, phone script, or any marketing and sales piece.

After you make a claim in your piece regarding the specific feature you offer in a product/service, consider these 4 words (credit to Dave Dee who I learned this from):

> *"Which means to you..."*

Just stating a feature is not enough to make it really stick in the heart of your prospect. You need to bring it down to the reality of how exactly that benefit matters to THEM.

For example, if you state:

> "I have over 30 years of experience creating marketing campaigns at Fortune 500 Companies all across the United States..."

You need to consider and add:

> "... which means to you you're not getting someone who just downloaded an e-book on Pay-Per-Click advertising. My years of experience have shown me exactly how to craft an integrated, multi-step marketing campaign that delivers exactly the right message at exactly the right time in the customer's journey from prospect to buyer. Every step in the process is anticipated and addressed - there's no risk to you for a disaster caused by someone who really doesn't know what they're doing."

Get the idea? No one cares about what you have to offer until you frame it in terms that matter to them.

Burn these 4 words into memory so you ALWAYS remember to factor them into every sales presentation from this point on.

81. USE A GRABBER TO CATCH THEIR ATTENTION

Here's another little tip to toss in your arsenal of power words, killer headlines, and sure-fire offers.

Grabbers

When you want to make a big impression in your sales letter, adding a grabber is one more way to add eye candy appeal.

A grabber is simply some kind of object you attach to your sales letter to create interest and attention. Then, you tie that grabber into the content of your opening headline. Here are a couple simple examples:

Tootsie Roll

"Hold On Tight, Because Here's a Sweet Deal That Will Roll You Over!"

Poker Chip

"Here's a Sure Fire Bet For Your Next Awards Banquet!"

Golf Tee

"Don't 'Drive' Yourself Nuts Trying to Find The Solution to Your Rodent Problem..."

You are only limited by your imagination - there are hundreds, if not thousands of different little items you could stick on a letter to create interest.

Open up your junk drawer, rummage around a bit, and brainstorm some creative letter openers of your own.

82. USE QUESTIONS TO WRITE FASTER

First, let's get this out of the way - you want to be able to write faster. The faster you can write, the faster you can produce sales copy, brochures, blog posts, webpages, postcards, emails - all of which can bring you in more moola.

Now you might be wondering... how can using questions help you write faster? Okay, consider how you'd write a response to both of these statements:

> *Describe the chair you're sitting in.*

Versus....

> *What do hate about that chair?*

World of difference, eh what?

No matter where you are in your level of expertise as a writer, you will write faster when you are respond to questions. A statement gives you too much leeway... too many ways to veer off the tracks. Too much freedom, which can and will lead to paralysis (i.e., writer's block!).

On the other hand, a question provides focus. It gives you something specific to hang your hat onto. So use the power of Who, What, When, Where, Why, and How as you frame your copy.

Here's a very practical application. The next time you write a sales letter, create the outline using questions, not statements. For example:

*** House Painter Sales Letter ***

You could start writing from...

- My Background
- Types of Painting I do
- References
- Packages

OR... you could use questions like...

- Why should you hire me to paint your house?
- What is my background as a house painter?
- What will I do while I'm at your home?
- What do previous customers say about me?
- What packages do I offer?

Use questions to shape and direct your writing. It will help you write faster, which saves time and gets YOU to the money sooner.

83. RECYCLE

When I say recycle, I'm talking about leveraging proven marketing pieces when creating new sales letters and promotional materials. One of the most valuable tools I have when writing sales copy is a big honking binder packed front to back with junk mail, sales letters, and other promotions I've saved over the years.

There are ads for financial newsletters, magazines, audios, record clubs, exercise equipment, doctors, health foods, and many many more. And if you want it, you'll have to pull it from my cold dead typing fingers ... it's that vital to my business.

There's so much gold in there - headlines, subheads, lead ins, bullet points, on and on and on. Not that I can take any them verbatim... no way, we deal in totally different markets and services... but the structure, the style, the formatting... all these provide incredibly useful examples to use when you sit down at the keyboard to knock out that next sales letter or website.

So the next time you face down the terror of a blank screen when crafting some kind of sales piece, take a leisurely stroll through your own stack of stashed sales letters and let your imagination roll.

It'll make the challenge of writing great copy a whole lot easier and lot more fun.

84. BRAINSTORM KEY WORDS AND KEY PHRASES

A major mistake just about every small biz makes is to bust tail to put up a website and then worry about getting traffic to it.

A much better approach is this:

1. Nail down exactly who you're aiming this website at.

2. Brainstorm the words and phrases this person would use to find your service on the web.

I'm presuming you've already done #1 - but #2 is something we all could put more focus on.

Keywords and keyword phrases are gold when it comes to keeping your sales site focused and easy to find. You will use them for the copy on the site, your Google Adwords campaign, and the tags you build into the underlying code of your webpage.

You'll also use them as associated tags for videos you upload about your services, with the image ALT tags, and so much more.

So don't delay. Do this. Get inside your prospect's head and think up what they'll use to find you.

85. SHORT AND SWEET SALESLETTER FORMULA

Here's a short and sweet Sales Letter formula you can use for your letters, your brochures, and especially your websites.

****

PreHead to Nail Down/Qualify the customer:

"Attention: Corporate Event Planners..."

Compelling headline the promises a clear benefit:

"How to..."

Dear Friend:

Short opening sentence that excites the curiosity.

State a major problem the customer is facing.

Establish your credibility as expert on that problem.

Tease that a solution is coming...

Offer up social proof in testimonials.

Answer objections the customer may have.

Restate problem and offer bullet points on how you'll solve them - these are the features and benefits of your service.

More proof in testimonials - reinforce what you've just said.

Establish scarcity in terms of your availability.

Clear call to action to therefore contact you now.

Signature

P.S., Offer a compelling bonus for contacting you immediately instead of waiting - price break, whatever.

Repeat call to action - contact me now!

****

86. CREATE A DO NOT OPEN ENVELOPE

Here's a marketing strategy that famed entertainer Johnny Carson, or more appropriately his alter-ego "Karnac the Great!", would have loved. It's called "the sealed envelope trick."

If you're sending out direct mail in a plain, personal looking envelope, try putting your brochures or your colorful flyers or other response pieces in another envelope. And on the outside of that envelope have printed, "Do not open this until you've read my letter."

Remember, if you're sending what looks like a personal letter, when your prospect opens the envelope they should see a letter.

If they open the envelope and they see your full-color brochure, they're going to be upset because you tricked them into opening up the envelope.

By putting that extra piece in another envelope, you're providing the backup sales oomph that you wanted, and you're doing it in a clever way that's bound to raise interest.

87. SHAKE 'EM UP

Ever watch TV with the hopes that maybe something... something... will wind up offering a hint of value?

Me too.

One morning, after grabbing a cuppa joe, I endured the morning news for a few minutes as I collected my thoughts for the day. During a commercial for gasoline, the following phrase popped out:

> *"Performance Robbing Gunk"*

After a pretty dry, technical dissertation on why their fuel was better than everyone else's, this nifty little ditty really rang out.

> *"Performance Robbing Gunk"*

Now that states the problem the customer faces directly and effectively. Who wants that crud clogging up their V8? Darn tooting, I don't!

It's a great mini-lesson in writing copy. All too often we settle for tired, worn-out cliche's that everyone's heard a thousand times before. We say the same stuff in the same way in the same sequence as everyone else. (My top pet peeve is "take it to the next level..." ARGH!)

So the copywriting hack here is simple:

Dare to differ and SHAKE 'EM UP!

Make bold assertions in your copy. Use vivid, vibrant words that shock the reader into actually noticing what you've written.

The numero uno sin for marketing materials is that they're boring boring boring. Same old, same old will get you same old same old results.

Create copy that's just as exciting, unique, and magical as you are.

88. THE LAZY WAY TO WRITE GREAT COPY

Here's how to be really lazy and still write great copy. Interested?

Over the past few weeks I've written a number of very successful sales pieces based on a shortcut method I'm going to teach you right now.

Step 1: Get a handle on who you're writing the letter to. This is probably the most critical step and you should NOT short cut the thinking you do here. Nuff said.

Step 2: Go to your swipe file and start browsing. You do have a swipe file, right? In case you're not sure, a swipe file is simply a collection of sales letters, display ads, websites, etc. that you've encountered that you think were really well done. This includes all the junk mail you've stashed from credit card companies, holistic health remedies, politicians, and so on. I have several huge binders PACKED with stuff like this. Hundreds and hundreds of pages.

Browse through this stack of ads until you find one that just has a flow and structure you like. Maybe you like the headlines and subheads. Maybe it's just about the right length. I don't know, just find one that feels about right to you.

Step 3: Write your sales letter based on the swipe file ad you picked out. Now, I'm not saying you copy it word for word. In fact, if they're selling hair-growth cream and you're promoting a mentalism show, odds are you'd probably confuse your prospect big time. What I am saying, however, is take those carefully crafted headlines, sentences, and paragraphs and rephrase them for you, your market, and your offer.

For example, one great way to do this is with the bullet points that describe the features of your program. Here's some examples from an ad written by master copywriter Gary Halbert:

- An amazing secret that can turn your local newspaper into your own personal goldmine.
- What to write on a cheap little postcard that will make people flood you with cash!
- How to use "976" phone numbers to get people to pay to hear your sales pitch!

Heck, I'm ready to buy already!

So, let's take these bullets and rewrite them for a magical sales training program you want to offer to local car dealerships.

- An amazing secret that turns the classic "penny from the kid's ear" trick into your own personal goldmine.
- What to write on a cheap little notepad that will convince your prospect you can literally see inside their minds and get them the deal they've always dreamed of!
- How to use a borrowed dollar bill and a pen in way that practically makes them beg to hear your sales pitch!

Get the picture? You don't copy what someone else has written ... you use it as inspiration to your own writing.

Just do this for the entire sales letter, following its basic outline and structure.

I love this technique and it can save you a ton of time and trouble ... a pretty handy way to make life a bit easier as you lazily head on down to that horizon

89. GET ANGRY AND START TYPING

Sometimes you'll just see something that totally pisses you off. One post on an online bulletin board totally got my goat. A guy was dissing me and others for using "ugly junk peddling websites" to sell their services.

I have some serious issues with that statement. So I had to respond. Here's what I said:

Who the hell ever said to put up an "ugly junk peddling website"!??

Eric never did. Dean never has. I certainly haven't.

You want to talk ugly, do a search on magician and be prepared for the crapola you'll find. Dorky graphics. Hokey music. Text you need a magnifying glass to read.

Or the other extreme... ultra slick, ultra cool, ultra flashy that takes days to load even on broadband and then never tells the customer what they want to know.

It's a rare "designer" who knows anything about making a sale. And that's exactly what your website is doing, it's a way to make a sale, pure and simple.

If you think it's anything else, or has any other purpose, then you are wasting server space and gumming up the internet with even more nonsense.

People are searching for solutions. Pack your website with answers to what your customers are looking for.

Harry Beckwith, in his great book "Selling the Invisible" makes an awesome point... the hardest thing in the world to sell is a service. There's no fancy car to drape Cindy Crawford all over. There's no "fresh minty scent" to tantalize the senses. And there's nothing under the hood to look at and pretend like you have any idea what that do-hickey means.

We're selling something that's totally amorphous and completely 100% trust-based. They have to trust us that we can solve their problems.

So no, don't put up an ugly, junk peddling website. I don't peddle junk, I offer quality solutions that surprise, engage, delight, and entertain. I bring joy into living rooms and board rooms. I make a positive contribution to peoples' lives and businesses.

And my websites work like hell to get that point across in a compelling, crystal-clear way. Period.

Ya know, I'm sure of it... I write my best stuff when I get mad. I'll bet you do too.

So get mad and write some hot-ass copy for your website today. People out there need you.

90. GET PERSONAL

It's good to get personal with your customers. Now I'm not talking anything awkward or inappropriate. What I mean is we need to talk to our customers in plain, straightforward, from-the-heart language.

Anything you send ... be it thank you, birthday card, newsletter, or sales piece...should read like it's just plain ol' you sitting across the table saying what's on your mind.

Great sales copy reads like a personal conversation from one to another. AWAI has a very good copywriting course with a whole book packed with great sales letters. One of the first assignments is to copy... by hand... a sales letter produced for American Express.

(By the way, that's a great tip... find a killer sales letter and write it out by hand a few times. It will really give you a gut-level understanding of how top notch copy ebbs and flows. Try it sometime!)

This AMEX letter reads like someone hanging out on the couch alongside you, chit-chatting about stuff that means something. It's a great example of copy that's direct, personal, and gets to the heart of what really matters to me... the reader.

Personal really means, more than anything, a flowing, conversational style that just feels like one guy talking to another. No high-falutin' language. No "let me impress you with my 10-dollar vocabularly"... just plain talk about stuff you care about.

(For instance, how to write better sales letters...:-)

Of course, you need to include the other stuff... an eye-catching headline that grabs attention, power-packed testimonials that back you up... but the core of all your sales copy writing should always focus on the "cut to thechase" bottom line business of speaking directly to your customer's needs - one to one.

91. PHOTO ENCLOSED

We're all curious George's on the inside. We all love a secret. We all love to get the inside dish.

Then why not apply that principle to your mailings?

You've heard the saying that "a picture is worth a thousand words" -- well today, I'm going to show you how a picture can be worth thousands and thousands of dollars. I don't know many people who are using this strategy, but the "photo enclosed" direct mail strategy is killer.

On the outside of the envelope have the words, "Photo Enclosed! Do Not Bend!' printed.

These words are going to get your envelope opened. Almost everyone opens the envelope to see what the photograph is.

Now, what should a photograph be? It could just be of you, you with your family or almost anything you can tie in with your sales letter.

A great strategy is to have a picture of yourself with one of your happy clients and also include a testimonial letter from that client talking about the great results he/she got from using your product or service.

Try this strategy. I think you'll like the results.

92. INCLUDE A REAL COUPON

Use a discount gift certificate tied in with a response deadline.

For example, let's say you charge $225.00 for a specific program. Send a coupon, good for $25.00 off the price that is only valid if the prospect calls and hires you before a certain date. This technique works great!

Make sure to send an actual coupon. Don't just write in your sales letter that you'll give them a discount. Tests show a coupon or gift certificate pulls much better than just saying you'll give a discount. (I've had great results printing this coupon on bright yellow card stock.).

93. MORE GRABBER IDEAS

Just a quick review. A grabber is something you attach to a letter or enclose with a letter that is designed to catch (grab) your reader's attention. You should definitely test using grabbers. They can really boost your response.

1. Aspirin ... "Christmas Party Planning Headaches? I Can Help You."
2. A Leaf ... "Don't Fall For Bargain Priced Entertainers That Leaf Your Audiences Bored And Unsatisfied."
3. A Match ... "A Really Hot Idea For Your Company Picnic."
4. Alka-Seltzer Package ... "Is Motivating Your Employees Giving You A Headache?"
5. Tea Bag ... "This Will Only Take You Three Minutes To Read So Sit Back, Relax, and Have A Cup Of Tea On Me."
6. Fake Banana ... "You're Driving Me Bananas! I've called you, written you, and begged you to get my free report, "10 Insider Secrets To Making Your Next Trade Show A Success"."
7. Mock Check/Gift Certificate ... "Rather than spend money on advertising, I've decided to give it to you in the form of this gift certificate.
8. Birthday Candle ... "Your Child's Birthday Is Around The Corner. Here's How To Make Her Party The Best Ever."
9. Balloon ... "As you can see, I've attached a balloon to the top of this letter. Why have I done this? Two reasons. First, I wanted to attract your attention. And second, what I have to say concerns how you can make your next corporate function unforgettable, exciting, and fun."
10. Magic Wand ... "The Secret To Making Your Corporate Entertainment Problems Disappear."

Give some of these a try and have fun!

94. KEEP IT SHORT AND SWEET

When writing sales copy, keep it simple, use precise language, and explain your offer in detail.

Keep your sentences short. No more than 17 words in a sentence.

95. WRITE IT OUT BY HAND

When you are writing copy, write out the first draft by hand. Virtually every great copywriter does that. (This was a new concept for me and it works.)

96. REPLACE THE SCARY WORDS

"In the beginning was the word..."

So says the good book. And words still matter. More than we can even imagine. Especially when we're talking with a prospect, whether in person or in print.

Choose your words with great care. Here's a few pointers with a grateful nod to "How To Master The Art Of Selling" by Tom Hopkins.

"BUY"

People don't like to buy things. They like to own things or they like to invest in things. Don't say to your client, "After you buy package # 1" instead say, "After you invest in package #1..."

"PRICE or COST"

These are scary words for a prospect. Don't say, "The price of my birthday party package is...". Instead say, "The total investment for my deluxe package is..." Sound nicer and more professional doesn't it?

"SIGN"

What did your mother tell you that you must do before you sign anything? That's right, "Read the whole thing". We're not trying sneak anything by our clients but when you want them to "sign" something ask them to "authorize," "endorse," or "approve" it.

"CONTRACT"

People don't like to endorse contracts. You need a lawyer to get out of a contract and that's scary. They will approve "Performance Agreements" though.

"PITCH"

"Let me come in and pitch you on this idea for your next meeting." How disgusting and insulting. You are a professional. You don't "pitch" ideas. You make "presentations" and "demonstrations" relative to "programs" you offer.

Think about the words you use the next time you're speaking with a prospect or writing a sales letter.

These may seem like small things, but they can add up big time to making you sound more professional and strengthening your marketing position.

97. MAKE SURE TO SET THE BUYING CRITERIA

This is perfect for lead generation and sales letters where you say something like "The 7 Key Questions to Ask Before Hiring a Plumber" – or insert any other profession or product.

You want to identify as "Key Questions" or "Key Reasons" aspects of your product or service that together only YOU can provide. You tie these to core features or aspects of what you offer or do... For instance, as a magician:

- I offered a money back guarantee. That made me different.
- I specialized in kidshows. Most magicians take any gig they can.
- I had full liability coverage. Ditto for most other magicians.
- I appeared as a Genie, not a "top-hat-and-tails" magician. Most magicians tried to look pretty standard.

These were elements of what my service offered. So I turned them all into critical criteria you as a customer needed in order to make a good buying decision, as in:

1. Don't hire any magician who doesn't offer a money-back guarantee.

2. Only hire kidshow specialists – you don't want "adult" or inappropriate humor at your child's party.

3. Don't hire any magician who doesn't carry full liability insurance – you need full protection.

4. Only hire an entertainer that stands out from the "boring crowd" of look-a-like entertainers. Get someone with personality and creativity.

Whenever you can, set the buying criteria clearly in your sales pitch.

98. WRITE LIKE YOU SPEAK

Don't try to write "formal" or "proper" English.

Just use your own natural writing voice; you have a natural voice that you use when speaking.

You already know how to speak, just say it. Put it down on paper.

Give it a solid look over to make sure you hit the key points you wanted. And then send it out and see what happens.

BEFORE YOU SEND IT "GUT CHECK" HACKS

(Hacks 99-101)

99. 10 POINT KILLER COPY CHECKLIST

Here's a handy and quick 10-point checklist for creating Killer Copy:

1. Decide what the outcome is going to be for you writing your copy. Are you trying to generate leads or make the sale? *This is a CRITICAL decision.*
2. Know the market and what your prospect wants.
3. Create a "FACT SHEET" about what you want to sell. Make it long, make it detailed, make it complete. You want to write down every detail.
4. Create a corresponding benefit list. (Translate the facts into benefits.)
5. Write down your killer offer
6. Write down lots of headlines.
7. Select a copywriting formula and write the first draft.
8. Put the copy aside for a day or two.
9. Read copy aloud and edit
10. Edit again

If you just follow this checklist with each sales letter you write, you will be miles ahead of 99% of your competition - because they don't consider this stuff important.

And you know it is.

100. DOUBLE CHECK YOUR PITCH

Every time you send out a mailing/flyer/business card/website/etc. it's needs to "pitch" something.

Maybe it's to call you.

Maybe it's to get them to provide their email address.

Maybe it's to get them to fill in Credit Card info and buy.

Regardless, you should always be telling your prospect with every element of marketing collateral you use to "DO" something.

Here are the elements every PITCH needs to have:

- A Headline that describes a clear benefit to the prospect.
- At least one-to-many testimonials from happy customers of your products/services.
- A specific OFFER that gives them a reason to contact you... this offer is conceived and phrased as being in the prospect's best interest.
- Something to drive that offer to make them act IMMEDIATELY - a time limit deadline, perhaps some kind of scarcity (e.g., only 10 available at that price!) or some bonus disappears.
- Multiple ways to contact you to take advantage of that offer - phone, email, etc.

These are NOT optional elements. Each and every one of them is REQUIRED... otherwise you haven't given your marketing its very best shot at success.

101. ASK THESE FOUR INCREDIBLE QUESTIONS

I'm a big fan of the classics, especially movies. Some of my favorite films date back to the golden age of cinema - when stars like Bogart, Cagney, Jimmy Stewart, and John Wayne lived large across the silver screen. Words became magic in the mouths of these masters.

And if you study the craft of screenwriting, you should absolutely grab copies of the classic movie scripts to study and learn from.

The same holds true for writing great sales copy. One master you may not know was a man named Maxwell Sackheim. Born in 1890 in Russia, Sackheim was a copywriting pioneer and creative genius who invented many of the long time successful concepts in direct marketing history. He's credited with writing the classic ad entitled: *"Do you make these mistakes in English?"* for Sherman Cody's English course, which ran for over 40 years.

Let me say, if I had an ad that cranked out profits for four decades, I would absolutely be one happy camper!

Here's some valuable questions from Sackheim that you may want to consider when crafting any sales piece. They boil down to four things you need to always remember:

1 - Why should anyone read or listen to it?

2 - Why should anyone believe it?

3 - Why should anyone do anything about it?

4 - Why should it be acted upon immediately?

Next time you write a salesletter, a webpage, a postcard, or even an email to your prospects, run through these questions first to see whether your copy has good answers for each.

Four questions. All simple. Each incredibly powerful.

ABOUT THE AUTHOR

For decades, I focused on growing my career as a writer (my very first stint was writing comedy for a college radio show with my friend Tim Allen). After graduation, I bounced around at different jobs across the country - Michigan, Texas, Boston - having a good run writing for high-tech companies.

But on my 50th birthday, I marched into my boss's office at Microsoft and told him "I'm quitting to become a magician."

Even though my job as game writer for Flight Simulator, Age of Empires, and multiple XBox titles had been a blast, I still wanted to go for my dream of making a living as a professional magician and entrepreneur.

It was quite the ride - with plenty of ups and downs along the way. I'm an excellent kidshow performer, but the magic of a successful business only became real after I discovered the power of direct response copywriting in the mold of Dan Kennedy, John Caples, and other copy greats. I extended my business to help other magicians successfully sell their services... through webinars, live events, and products.

Eventually, my success as a marketer and copywriter led me to join Dan Kennedy's company - GKIC - where for over three years I led the copy team as Head Copywriter. Now I provide marketing / writing services and counsel to a variety of clients in many different industries.

As you might imagine, I'm not afraid to travel a different path - you only live once, why not make it an experience...

For more information, check out my website:

www.YouDontNeedACopywriter.com

Made in the USA
San Bernardino, CA
21 November 2018